D0886748

The 1973 Pere Marquette
Theology Lecture

AMBIGUITY
IN
MORAL CHOICE

by

Richard A. McCormick, S. J.

Marquette University Press
Milwaukee, Wisconsin 53233

ISBN 0-87462-505-X

Second Printing 1977

© Copyright 1973
Marquette University Press
Milwaukee, Wisconsin, U.S.A.

The distinction between what is directly voluntary and indirectly voluntary has been a staple of Catholic moral thought for centuries.[1] It has been used to face many practical conflict-situations where an evil can be avoided or a more or less necessary good achieved only when another evil is reluctantly caused. In such situations the evil caused as one goes about doing good has been viewed as justified or tolerable under a fourfold condition. (1) The action is good or indifferent in itself; it is not morally evil. (2) The intention of the agent is upright, that is, the evil effect is sincerely not intended. (3) The evil effect must be equally immediate causally with the good effect, for otherwise it would be a means to the good effect and would be intended. (4) There must be a proportionately grave reason for allowing the evil to occur. If these conditions are fulfilled, the resultant evil was referred to as an "unintended byproduct" of the action, only indirectly voluntary and justified by the presence of a proportionately grave reason.[2]

The practical importance of this distinction can be gathered from the areas where it has been applied in decision-making:　killing (self–defense, warfare, abortion, euthanasia, suicide), risk to life (dangerous missions, rescue operations, experimentation), sterilization, contraception, sexual reactions, cooperation in another's evil action, scandal. Its appeal is attested to by the long line of prominent theologians who have used it in facing problems of the first magnitude such as the conduct of war. The most articulate contemporary exponent of the just war theory (Paul Ramsey) appeals to it frequently in his writings[3] much as did John C. Ford, S.J. in his excellent work on obliteration bombing.[4]　Many other theologians fall back on the distinction, sometimes unwittingly, sometimes when it suits a rather obvious purpose.　So settled, indeed, had the usage become in theological circles that the direct–indirect distinction has achieved a decisive prominence in some of the most influential and authoritative documents of the Church's magisterium.

For instance, in discussing the problem

of abortion, Pius XI asked: "What could ever be a sufficient reason for excusing in any way the direct murder of the innocent (**directam innocentis necem**)."[5] Pius XII **repeatedly** condemned the "deliberate and **direct** disposing of an innocent human life"[6] and insisted that "neither the life of the mother nor that of the child can be subjected to an act of **direct** suppression."[7] Similarly Pius XII employed the distinction in dealing with sterilizing drugs. He noted that "if the wife takes this medication not with a view to preventing conception, but solely on the advice of a physician, as a necessary remedy by reason of a malady of the uterus or of the organism, she is causing an **indirect** sterilization, which remains permissible according to the general principle concerning actions having a double effect. But one causes a **direct** sterilization, and therefore an illicit one, whenever one stops ovulation in order to preserve the uterus and the organism from the consequences of a pregnancy which they are not able to stand."[8]

Where the conduct of war is concerned,

recent documents of the magisterium have insisted on what theologians refer to as non-combatant immunity or the principle of discrimination. Thus Pius XII, after stating that an aggrieved nation may licitly turn to warfare as a last defensive resort, immediately rejected a use of nuclear weapons which "entirely escapes from the control of man" and represents "the pure and simple annihilation of all human life within the radius of action."[9] The Second Vatican Council condemned as a crime against God and man "any act of war aimed indiscriminately at the destruction of entire cities . . ."[10] The principle of discrimination proposed in such statements has commonly been explained and applied through the distinction direct-indirect.[11]

In 1968 Pope Paul VI made explicit use of the distinction between direct and indirect in **Humanae Vitae**. He stated: "We must once again declare that the **direct** interruption of the generative process already begun, and above all, **directly** willed and procured abortion, even if for therapeutic reasons, are to be absolutely excluded as licit means of regulating birth."[12] He immediately added: "Equally to be excluded, as the teaching authority of the Church has frequently declared, is **direct** sterilization, whether perpetual or temporary, whether of the man or of the woman."

More recently the "Ethical and Religious Directives for Catholic Hospitals," approved overwhelmingly by the American bishops in November 1971, refers repeatedly to the distinction between direct-indirect. Directive 10 reads: "The directly intended termination of any patient's life, even at his own request, is always morally wrong."[13] Similarly, prohibited abortion is described as "the **directly** intended termination of pregnancy before viability." Furthermore, the revised Directives define what direct must be taken to mean: "Every procedure whose sole immediate effect is the termination of pregnancy before viability is an abortion."

It is safe to say, therefore, that the rule of double effect has had an honored and very important place in the formulation of Catholic moral theology and teaching.

However, in the past four or five years,[14] there have been rumblings of dissatisfaction, uncertainty, disagreement—or all three. These sentiments have surfaced in several studies which reapproach the distinction between direct and indirect, to test its traditional understanding, to challenge its decisiveness, or even to deny its moral relevance. Clearly we have here an issue of the greatest theoretical and practical importance, one that deserves most careful reflection. The purpose of this essay is to review critically several recent studies on direct–indirect voluntariety and to offer some personal reflections in an attempt to identify the present state of the moral question.

It should be said at the outset that these reflections should be regarded as no more than gropings and explorations undertaken with the confidence that others more competent will carry them further and bring greater clarity to the question. A distinction with a history as imposing and long-lived as that between the direct and indirect voluntary should not be abandoned unless its inadequacy is rather clearly and systematically established. I say this because in these our times there are far too many ready and eager to turn a theological question into a new discovery, and to promulgate this **urbi et orbi** in terms which the professional theologian can only regret, and most often disown completely.

The recent discussion was, I believe, largely put in motion by the writings of Peter Knauer, S.J.[15] Knauer, it will be recalled, began with the insistence that moral evil consists in the permission or causing of a physical evil without commensurate reason. In explaining this, Knauer relied heavily on St. Thomas' analysis of self-defense. The defense of one's life against an assailant is not exactly an effect, but rather an aspect of the act. Therefore, the **finis operis** or meaning of an action is not derived simply from its external effect but is really that aspect of the act which is willed. For example, almsgiving is not simply a physical act; it gets its sense and becomes a moral act through the intention of the donor.

Knauer argues that it is with this in mind that we must understand the terms "direct" and "indirect." In the past we have tied these terms too closely to physical causality.[16]   Actually, "the permission or causing of a physical evil is direct or indirect as there is or is not present a commensurate reason," for when such a reason is present, it "occupies the same area as what is directly willed and alone determines the entire moral content of the act.   If the reason of an action is commensurate, it alone determines the **finis operis**, so that the act is morally good."[17]

What, then, is a commensurate reason? This is crucial to Knauer's presentation. It is not just any reason, meaningful or important as it may be. Rather a reason is commensurate if the value realizable here and now by measures involving physical evil in a premoral sense is not in the long run undermined and contradicted by these measures but supported and maximized. Thus "a refusal to bear children is only commensurately grounded if it is ultimately in the interests of the otherwise possible child."[18]   Or again, "to prove that a particular act is contraceptive in the moral sense it must be shown that the act in the last analysis does not serve the end of preservation and deepening of marital love, but in the long run subverts it."[19]

To the objection that this amounts to proposing that a good end justifies an evil means, Knauer would reply that a means can be judged to be evil only if it is caused without commensurate reason. One cannot, in other words, isolate certain physical evils and say of them that they are, in all circumstances, moral evils. The distinction between physical and moral evil is not, of course, new. For instance, in discussing the principle that a good end does not justify an evil means, the late and renowned Gerald Kelly, S.J., wrote:

> This principle, so simple in itself, can be very complicated in its explanation. It does not mean that no evil may be done in order to obtain good. It refers primarily to **moral** evil; and in this respect it is absolute, because **moral** evil may never be done to obtain any kind of good.

The principle is not absolute as re-
gards **physical** evil, because there are
some physical evils that we have a
right to cause in order to obtain a
good effect.   An example of this
latter that is very common in medicine is mutilation. Mutilation is certainly a physical evil; yet as we shall
see, there are some circumstances in
which man has a right to mutilate
himself or to authorize such mutilation."20

This explanation of Kelly is absolutely
correct.   What is not clear is what is to
count (and why) for **moral** evil.   Kelly
clearly regarded contraceptive interventions and directly sterilizing interventions,
for example, as falling in this category.
Knauer has questioned—and I believe
rightly—just that type of conclusion and
insisted that what is morally evil can only
be determined after we have examined the
reason for the procedure.   What is to be
said of Knauer's understanding of direct
and indirect intent?   My earlier reaction
was critical.   Since that time, however, I
have come to accept the substance of
Knauer's presentation, though not without serious qualifications about his use of

the terms "direct" and "indirect" as will become clear in the course of this study.

Germain Grisez says of Knauer that he "is carrying through a revolution in principle while pretending only a clarification of traditional ideas."[21]   As Grisez sees it, Knauer's basic failing is that he overlooks a very important mode of obligation. He "ignores the obligation that we not turn directly against the good. This omission opens the way for his redefinition of 'directly intended' in a way that bears no relation to any previous use of the expression. To support his position, Knauer also finds it necessary to claim that moral intent is completely distinct from psychological intent."[22]

I shall discuss later the notion of "turning directly against the good" as proposed by Grisez.   However, his criticism of Knauer's neglect of psychological intent is, I believe, justified. The notions of "direct" and "indirect" intention have become so utterly identified with the existence of a commensurate reason in Knauer's thought that "direct" and "indirect" really do not function. This is not

to deny the decisive nature of commensurate reason or to challenge the substance
of Knauer's approach. It is only to note
that Knauer seems to give no meaning to
psychological intent. One can only won-
der why Knauer retained the terminology
at all. Secondly, Knauer does not satis-
factorily indicate the limitations of intention in determining the meaning of concrete human actions and therefore he is
unable to deal convincingly with cases like
that of Mrs. Bergmeier who committed
adultery to free herself from prison and
rejoin her family.[23]

The next theologian to turn a critical
eye to the direct-indirect distinction was
William Van der Marck.[24] His critique is
intelligible only within the larger frame-
work of his thought. Van der Marck's
treatment is anchored in the notion of
intersubjectivity. He notes:

> The fact that human action is inter-
> subjective means that it necessarily
> has consequences favorable or detri-
> mental to the mutual relationship of
> the persons concerned. To state this
> more directly, intersubjectivity is a
> form of either communication or the

disruption of communication; it is a
form of either community or the
destruction of community. When we
now speak of act and consequences,
of act and effect, of means and end,
we are, in the first place, not speaking of something that happens **now**
and has results, consequences, or
effects, or that achieve an end **later**;
rather, we are speaking of a particular corporeal action that, precisely as
a human act, has immediate implications with respect to the relationship
between subjects.[25]

Now the essential meaning of "good" and
"evil" is simply a qualification of the
implications, effects, consequences. In
other words, it is only a qualification of
the human content of the act. Good and
evil, he insists, refer to the success or failure of intersubjectivity, "and for this
reason there cannot be any question of
good and evil unless there is first a question of intersubjectivity; furthermore, we
may speak of good and evil only to the
extent that we speak of intersubjectivity."
Van der Marck feels that the disease of
traditional moral theology is that it began
to maneuver among categories of good and

evil before it touched intersubjectivity.
Thus traditional theology would characterize something as a means and a bad one
prior to consideration of intersubjectivity.
For example, it would say that to have
children is good, but artificial insemination
is a bad means to it.

Van der Marck does not deny the use-
fulness of the categories object-circum-
stances, means-end. But he argues that
the "reality itself, however, is much more
important than categories and the tools
they provide, and when we do gain insight
into the reality itself, these categories and
other ways of approach will themselves
become more intelligible."[26]   Thus Van
der Marck sets out to criticize the categories in light of the reality.

What is the reality of man? Man is
both corporeal and intersubjective. "Cor-
porality qualifies man under all aspects in
which he coincides with and forms part of
the non-human world." Intersubjectivity,
on the other hand, points him out in his
human uniqueness. Now if this is true of
man, it is true of his action also. Therefore, the most fundamental thing to be

said about human action is the distinction between corporeity and intersubjectivity. Human action is a reality which is wholly corporeal, yet we see its uniqueness only when we view it as intersubjective.

A few examples offered by Van der Marck will throw light on his analysis. The physical, bodily reality of killing can be, as an intersubjective reality, murder, waging war, administering the death penalty, self-defense, suppressing an insurrection and so on. Taking something from another can be intersubjectively stealing, borrowing, satisfying dire need, repossessing one's property. Removing a nonviable fetus from the womb can be intersubjectively abortion (murder), removal of the effects of rape, saving the life of the mother and so on. Van der Marck feels that too often the reality of action is identified with one single form of intersubjectivity to the total exclusion of others. Why? Because the qualification "good" and "bad" is derived from the corporeal act as such, the physical act, in spite of the explicitly made distinction between **esse physicum** and **esse morale**.

The criticism he levels against traditional manuals of moral theology is this: "That the same material, bodily act may possibly have a **different** intersubjective significance is something that, in principle, lies outside its field of vision."[27]

Van der Marck then applies the corporeity–intersubjectivity distinction to the means–end and act–intention categories. Thus, means is related to end in the same way as corporeity is related to intersubjectivity. That is, just as intersubjectivity is the ultimate determinant of **human** action, so the end is the ultimate determinant of **human** action. "For example, termination of pregnancy could be called 'means,' and intersubjectivity would be indicated by 'end,' whether it be murder, removal of the effects of rape, or saving the life of the mother." Similarly with act (object) and intention. "Act refers to the whole action as a physiological reality, while intention refers to the same action, but precisely as human and intersubjective." In summary, intersubjectivity demands special consideration before we can speak about good and evil, for "what is material

in human action is able to be intersubjective in the most diverse and varied of
ways."28

Against this background, Van der Marck
approaches the principle of double effect.
The double effect principle is very helpful,
according to Van der Marck, in overcom-
ing the tendency to ascribe a meaning to
an action independent of intersubjectivity.
For the double effect principle, in distinguishing between action and effects, thereby distinguishes between corporeity and
intersubjectivity. However, the problem
with the principle according to Van der
Marck, is that "a twofold intersubjectivity
is ascribed to the act (two effects) and
then one aspect is immediately canceled
out ('indirectly willed' for 'sufficient reason')."29

According to him, both effects or aspects constitute the intersubjectivity of
the act, its human meaning. They are
there and are determinative of the meaning (and morality) of the act whether I
will them or not. To hold that one is only
indirectly willed (unintended) he sees as
"canceling it out."30 And he seems to

find that objectionable. What Van der Marck approves in the double effect idea is not, then, its validity as an adequate account of the human meaning (and morality) of our actions, but rather the fact that it moves a step away from assigning meaning independently of intersubjectivity. For effects are the intersubjective aspects of acts and to take them seriously is to take intersubjectivity seriously.

Ultimately, then, Van der Marck would abandon the distinction between direct and indirect. It is not an adequate tool to get at the meaning of our actions, and for two reasons, if I understand him correctly. First, it "cancels out" as indirect one aspect of intersubjectivity—the evil effect. Secondly, the morality of our actions requires a larger setting than that present in the assessment of immediate effects—that of community-building or destruction of community. Every action, as an intersubjective reality, is either a form of community or destruction of it. That **determines** its objective moral quality. "To call something 'good' or 'evil' is therefore, in the first instance, a highly prag-

matic statement that can be made only after the event, after one has been able to establish the 'results' actually produced by the action."[31]

Van der Marck's argument is basically this: we must first describe our conduct and its meaning in categories which respect our social nature before speaking of this conduct as good or evil. The conduct so described is then judged to be good or evil depending on whether it is community-building or not. This judgment is not adequately elaborated out of the categories of direct and indirect intent. His analysis, while a helpful corrective at key points, reveals, I believe, the symptoms and problems of a reaction. I see three serious problems in his approach.

The first difficulty raised by Van der Marck's analysis is the problem of the application of the categories corporeity–intersubjectivity to the categories of-means–end and act–intention, and the implications of this application. As for the application itself, the author says: means and end are formally, not materially distinct. They are related to each other just

as corporeity and intersubjectivity. Therefore, it is the end which contributes human meaning to action. This is true, it
seems, with regard to those "effects"
which are rather the immediate implications of one's activity than genuine, later-
on effects. Van der Marck is aware of this
distinction. For in writing of means–end,
act–effect, he says: "When we now speak
of act and consequences, of act and effect,
of means and end, we are, in the first
place, not speaking of something that happens **now** and has results, consequences,
rather, we are speaking of a particular
corporeal action that, precisely as a human
act, has immediate implications with respect to the relationship between 'subjects'."[32]   Therefore he does distinguish
"later–on effects" from "immediate implications." It is these latter which are
only formally distinct from the action and
which give human significance to my
action.

But how does one make this distinction
in practice? Perhaps "saving the life of
the mother" is not a "later–on" effect,
but an "immediate implication" of the

action giving it its basic human description and meaning. But Van der Marck has given us no satisfactory criterion for distinguishing the two. Grisez, as I shall indicate later, uses the criterion of indivisibility. But as I understand him, Van der Marck gives none. In other words, perhaps a case can be made for saying that terminating pregnancy to save the mother is actually not a use of a means to achieve an end, a means-to-end act. Rather the saving of the mother is an immediate implication of the act, its "intersubjectivity." Van der Marck should have attempted to show why in this instance we are not dealing with a true means at all, but with the immediate intersubjective implications of an act which define its basic human meaning. If one fails to do this, then eventually any intended effect can be grouped under title of end and be said to specify the act in its human meaning. In summary, there is a cutoff point between the physiological description of the action and the consequentialist (or intentional) description. It is this cutoff point that is not clear in Van der Marck. And it

is this cutoff point, I think, that is precisely the practical problem.

Secondly, there is the matter of "canceling out" the evil effect. "Canceling
out" is terribly loose theological language
and it is not clear what Van der Marck
intends by it. But it seems to convey the
idea of "not counting, ignoring." I do not
believe that the evidence justifies the statement that the rule of double effect was
denying that one aspect (the evil) of the
action had intersubjective significance. To
say that it was "canceled out" by indirectness implies this. The rule was rather insisting on just the contrary, and for this
reason demanding a truly proportionate
reason. If the evil effect had been "canceled out" by use of the double effect, no
proportionate reason would have been
demanded. One can argue that Van der
Marck's fear of a merely physiological
analysis of the meaning of an act has
brought him to a contrary extreme—
where physiological realities are totally
dominated by intent, and therefore, where
he is the one who cancels out the evil.
For instance, to redescribe emptying the

womb of a nonviable fetus as "destroying or removing the effects of rape" could be a rather hasty way of depersonalizing the fetus. The intention is, indeed, removing the effects of rape. But the most immediate, obvious, irrevocable implication of this removing is the destruction of nascent life. The language of intention dare not disguise this fact and suffocate the full implications of our conduct. To be consistent intersubjectivity must include all the subjects and the fetus cannot be that easily verbalized out of significance. We may characterize the action as "removing the effects of rape," but the question remains: is this morally appropriate when these effects are a person, or nascent human life?

The third problem is the criterion of community-building. There is, of course, a sense in which one cannot quibble with such a criterion. That is, if an action is, in its **full** intersubjective reality, eventually destructive of community, then clearly it is immoral and any criterion which approves it is inadequate. But at this point one asks: has experience and

reflection given us no practical presumptive judgments about what is community-building? I think it has. Van der Marck suggests the contrary when he says that good and evil are pragmatic statements "that can be made only after the event." Clearly we have more to learn, but by that same token we have learned something already. We know, for instance, that killing of others is, except in the most extreme and tragic circumstances, destructive of the **humanum** in every way, and is therefore destructive of community. And there are other things that we know before the event. Otherwise experience and reflection generate nothing by way of valid (I do not say exceptionless) generalization. In summary, if in the past we have identified good and evil too narrowly with the physical structure of the action, Van der Marck has backed off so far from this shortcoming that intention seems to swallow up the physical reality of the action. A balance is missing.

Another interesting discussion of the principle of double effect is that of Cornelius J. Van der Poel, C.S.SP.[33] His

thought-structure is very close to that of
Van der Marck. Van der Poel believes
that the standard interpretation of the
double effect has two weaknesses. First,
it fragments the human action. For instance, in the tragic case where termination of pregnancy is the only way to save
the mother's life, traditional casuistry has
spoken of the "direct killing" of the child
in order to save the mother. Van der Poel
rejects this as the proper reading of what
is going on. He notes: "The termination
of the pregnancy is seen as a negative
value, the saving of the mother as positive.
One effect viewed as a completely independent human act in itself seems to be
weighed against the other effect, also
viewed as a completely independent human act in itself. . . . Thus we get the
impression that the unity of the human
act of saving the mother (which includes
the most regrettable but inseparably con-
nected element of the death of the child)
is divided into two independent realities."[34]   Obviously, the thought of Van
der Marck hovers over this rendering.

Secondly, the traditional understanding

overemphasizes the importance of the **physical** effect in judging the **moral** value of the human action. Thus, in determining what is directly intended, moralists narrowed their focus too much to the physical structure of the act. If the **finis operis** of the act was killing, then that action was direct killing. The weakness of this approach was manifested, Van der Poel believes, in the moral discussion of organ transplants. Transplantation of organs demands the "direct" physical excising of an organ from the donor. However, this physical structure of the action must be put into its total context. "The physical excision of the organ is a part of the total human action of transplantation. The example shows that the physical structure of the act is merely a premoral consideration, and not itself determinant of morality."[35]

Thus physical occurrences which represent intermediate stages of a human action get **moral** determination from the totality of the human action. What gives this totality or unity? "The total intention or reason of the action." It is pre-

cisely this intention or purpose which
unites the intermediate stages and makes
the action **human**.   For example, "the
human action of surgical intervention . . .
is in its totality[36]   directed toward the
saving of the mother's life."

At this stage of his analysis Van der
Poel makes two important points. First,
not any material effect can be used to
obtain a good result.   There must be a
proportionate reason which makes the
occurrence of physical evil acceptable
within the whole act. Thus of an abortion
to avoid shame or inconvenience, Van der
Poel says that these purposes enter "into
the act of terminating the pregnancy" and
are the goals that "determine the human
meaning of it."   But they are (I presume
he 'would say, though he nowhere says it)
disproportionate, not sufficient to render
the evil caused acceptable.

Secondly, the intermediate stages within a total action are certainly voluntary
but they are "willed only in relation to
the purpose." The agent wills and wants
"the means of the intermediate stages
only insofar as the final goal **is contained**

in these means." Van der Poel gives the example of a person who loves nature and beauty and wants to view the countryside from the highest mountain peak in the area. The climb is long, fatiguing and perhaps dangerous. But the inseparable fatigue and danger do not constitute a separate object of the will. "There is only one object, the vision, which communicates its meaning to all the intermediate stages of the one **human** act." If we consider the fatiguing and dangerous climb as an independent entity we rob it of its specific **human** determination and ascribe a human value to an abstract physical entity.

This same analysis should be applied, he argues, to those actions which have a double effect. Thus, "the amputation of a leg may be an absolute requirement for the life and health of a person. In such a case the act of the will directs itself not to two different actions of amputation and cure, but the one act of curing includes the amputation unavoidably and defines the **human** meaning of the amputation itself."[37] In all such instances, we should not speak of an effect which is in **itself evil** but which can be "permitted." For that ascribes a human meaning to the material effect independent of the total human action. Thus, once we concentrate our attention on the total human action and the proportion between the evil caused (means) and the purpose (end) within this single action, we need not speak of direct and indirect willing. Rather the evil is voluntary *in se sed non propter se*.

Van der Poel, therefore, rejects the classical methodology that would face conflict situations by appeal to the notions of direct and indirect. But the question remains: how do we know whether the end or good of the action is proportionate to the evil caused within it? Here Van der Poel states that the "ultimate moral criterion is the community-building or destroying aspect of the action." Thus "the means for a particular action may never be so grave that the total result of the whole action would be damaging for the community."[38]

Van der Poel's analysis raises several problems. For instance, when are occur-

rences (of evil) to be viewed as only intermediate stages of a single action? May
every premoral evil that occurs in any way
in conjunction with my activity be re-
duced to an "intermediate stage?" For
example, is the killing of innocent children to get at the enemy's morale simply
an "intermediate stage" of the action
describable as "national self-defense"?
What is the criterion here? Somewhat
similarly, because it seems legitimate to
intend some premoral evils **in se sed non
propter se**, does it follow that all evils
which occur in conjunction with one's
activity can be said to be intended **in se
sed non propter se**? For instance, does
one intend and choose the death of the
fetus in a cancerous–uterus–situation in
the same way one intends and chooses
the fatigue and danger involved in a mountain climb? This can be doubted, as I will
attempt to show later. How one "intends"
premoral evil would seem to depend on
how that evil relates to the action—whether as effect, aspect, or integral and inseparable means.

It is, however, the matter of proportionate reason to which I wish to attend here. Van der Poel seems quite ambiguous on what this term should mean. When he says that not any good will justify any evil, he seems to suggest that proportionate reason is found in a balancing of the identifiable values immediately at stake. For instance, one may not abort a pregnancy simply to avoid shame. Yet at another point, he backs off from such a calculus and insists that "there needs to be a proportionate reason which makes the occurrence of the physical evil acceptable **in view of the total human existence.**" [39] Or again: "This total human action should be projected against the background of the whole of human existence in this world, to see whether it is contributing to it or destructive in its results." [40] The evil in the action "may never be so grave that the total result of the whole action would be damaging for the community." Briefly, the proportionate reason is determined by whether the action is community-building or not.

Van der Poel is, I believe, both right and wrong. First the good news. Obviously—

as was pointed out above where Van der Marck is concerned—if an action is reasonably foreseen or eventually known to be ultimately community–damaging, it is, regardless of its immediate meaning and rewards, immoral. The criterion is clearly correct in this rear–view–mirror sense. But now for the bad news. To propose as the only criterion of the morality of an act a measure so utterly ultimate is to suggest (at least) that more proximate criteria are useless or invalid. That is, in my judgment, to bypass a good deal of accumulated experience and wisdom. Furthermore, pastorally it is a general invitation to creeping exceptionism and to all kinds of self–serving and utilitarian decisions under the guise of community–building.

The problem, then, is not the validity of the ultimate criterion of community–building. It is rather the existence of more proximate norms. For instance, Van der Poel says: "When the life of the mother is certainly threatened by the fetus, the moralist (following the community–building criterion) can conclude to the taking of the life of the fetus in these circum-

stances."[41]   Just how **that** criterion leads
to **this** conclusion remains almost totally
mysterious. This is not to deny the conclusion, not at all. It is only to say that
unless one specifies a bit what counts for
community-building and how we know
this, then that criterion can be squeezed
to yield almost any conclusion—for instance, the immorality of all abortions, or
the morality of abortion on demand.

A criterion is like a weapon. If not
carefully and precisely constructed, it can
impale its user. This has happened, I believe, to Van der Poel. Speaking of self-
defense, he says: "We do not weigh the
independent value of the human life of
the unlawful attacker against the independent value of the life of the person who
legitimately defends himself against the
attack. We place the total action in the
social setting of human existence and we
call the whole action morally good provided that this was the only way to defend
himself."[42]   Here Van der Poel is left
dangling helplessly on his own **petitio
principii**. For the precise point of his
own criterion is not whether "this was the

only way to defend himself," but whether self–defense in such desperate circumstances is community–building or not. I believe self–defense is a legitimate Christian response. And I know of no studies that tell us that this response is more "community–building" than its opposite. Once again, I believe that behind this difficulty in Van der Poel is an over–reaction. His legitimate dissatisfaction with a narrow physicalism has led him to presume too readily that once he has shown that an action ought to be viewed and described as mother–saving, self–defense, or transplantation, it is community–building. It may be, but that is precisely the issue.

Against Van der Poel, I think we must also and first wrestle realistically with proportion in much narrower terms. That is, if the more immediate good achieved by the total act itself is not at least proportionate to the evils within it or accompanying it, then we must conclude that the action will be **de facto** community–damaging. This type of calculus could turn out to be shortsighted and wrong. But it should not be overlooked. For instance, if the purpose of a truly dangerous mountain climb is simply a view of natural beauty, one might easily conclude (in lack of other criteria) that such a climb represents an unjustified risk and is immoral. If, however, the same climb and same danger is undertaken to rescue another, a different assessment of proportion would be in place. Van der Poel himself suggests, perhaps unwittingly, that we need not always go foraging in the "community-building" forest but that the morality of an action which causes premoral evil can be found in a less sweeping and more modest criterion. In dealing with abortion of a pregnancy to avoid shame or burden or an unwanted child—an abortion I presume he considers immoral—he says: "The ultimate goal (in this case avoidance of shame or burden) enters into the act of terminating the pregnancy. It is this goal, therefore, that determines the human meaning of it."[43]   Granted, the intention does shade meaning.   But the question remains: is an action with this meaning morally acceptable?   If he considers the act immoral (as he seems to), it can only be because there is no proportion between "avoiding shame or burden" and destroying fetal life. The perception of this disproportion is not secured by reference to community-building or destroying. Indeed, it seems clear that anyone who does such disproportionate things does **thereby** something that is likely to be community-destroying.

Philippa Foot approaches the double effect from a different perspective.[44] After admitting the legitimacy of the distinction between "direct intention" and "oblique (or indirect) intention," she claims that the distinction plays only a very subsidiary role in determining what is right in difficult conflict situations. Much more important is the distinction between avoiding injury and bringing aid, a negative duty and a positive duty. The former weighs on us more strictly than the latter.

Foot uses several examples to illustrate her thesis. First there is the case of a runaway tram which the driver can steer only on either of two tracks. Five men are working on one track, only one on the other. Anyone working on either track is bound to be killed if the tram comes through. The second example, is that of a group of rioters demanding that a culprit be found for a certain crime and threatening to kill five hostages if he is not. The real culprit being unknown, the judge sees himself as able to prevent the death of five by framing one innocent person and having him executed. Foot says that we would unhesitatingly steer the tram down the track where it killed but one rather than five. But we would balk at framing one innocent man to save five. "Why can we not argue from the case of the steering driver to that of the judge?"

To that question Foot admits that the double effect provides an answer. The death of the innocent man framed by the judge would have to be intended. Whereas if he refrained, the deaths of the hostages would be unintended by him. But she believes that such situations should be solved in another way: by distinguishing positive and negative duties. In both cases we have a conflict of duties, but the steering driver faces a conflict of **negative** duties. His duty is to avoid injuring five men and his duty is also to avoid injuring one. "It seems clear he should do the least injury he can." The judge, however, is weighing the duty of not inflicting injury (negative) against the duty of bringing aid (positive). If our only choice is between conflicting negative duties or conflicting positive duties, we reasonably opt for the least harm or most good. But when the conflict is between negative (inflicting injury) and positive (bringing aid) we do not inflict injury to bring aid.

This is a thoughtful and intriguing study. I would agree with Foot that the double effect probably plays a lesser role in at least some conflict decisions than we have thought. Furthermore, her distinction between positive and negative duties is certainly valid and meaningful, although it is not new. It has been known for centuries. But tidy as it is, it still leaves unanswered questions. First of all, in applying the distinction to the case of abortion to save the mother (where nothing can be done to save mother and child, but where the mother can be saved), Foot states that "it is reasonable that the action that will save someone should be done." I would agree, but it is not clear how the distinction between bringing aid and avoiding injury functions here. Presumably Foot would say that abortion in this instance is "bringing aid." However, it is precisely the contention of traditional moralists that taking the child in this instance is "causing injury," even though the child is to perish. Foot nowhere shows why the operation should not be called "causing injury." Similarly, it is difficult to see how Foot would argue the moral legitimacy of self-defense and warfare if her overarching categories are "bringing aid" and "avoiding injury."

Secondly, and more importantly, Foot states that her "conclusion is that the distinction between direct and oblique intention plays only a quite subsidiary role in determining what we say in these cases, while the distinction between avoiding injury and bringing aid is very important indeed." What is this "subsidiary role?" This is not clear. Indeed, it would seem that it is ultimately no role at all. For at one point she states: "If you are permitted to bring about the death of the child, what does it matter how it is done?" If Foot had clarified the moral role of intention in human conflict situations, perhaps she would have clarified **why** and therefore **where** it is or is not permissible to inflict injury to bring aid. Not having done so, she retreats to the statement that "to refrain from inflicting injury ourselves is a stricter duty than to prevent other people from inflicting injury." Is it? That is precisely the point.

One of the most ranging and profound recent discussions of the double effect is that of Germain Grisez.[45] Grisez's analysis is developed with relentless consistency and subtlety. His treatment of the distinction between direct and indirect intention interlocks logically with his overall moral theory. This moral theory is developed somewhat as follows. The basic human goods (life, knowledge pursued for its own sake, interior integrity, justice, friendship, etc.) present themselves as goods-to-be-realized. They appeal to us for their realization. Thus these goods are the non-hypothetical principles of practical reason. "As expressions of what is-to-be, the practical principles present basic human needs as fundamental goods, as ideals."[46] But the appeal of these goods is not the direct determinant of moral obligation. They clarify the possibilities of choice but do not determine why some choices are morally good and others evil.

What determines this? The attitude with which we choose. What, then, is a right attitude? A realistic one. "To choose a particular good with an appreciation of its genuine but limited possibility and its objectively human character is to choose it with an attitude of realism."[47] The right attitude does not seek to belittle the good that is not chosen, but only seeks to realize what is chosen. This open, realistic attitude shapes itself into specific moral obligations. For instance, we must take all the goods into account in our deliberations; we must avoid ways of acting which inhibit the realization of any one of the goods to the extent possible; we must contribute our effort to their realization in others. A final and most

important mode of obligation is this: we
must never act "in a way directly destructive of a realization of any of the basic
goods." For to act **directly** against a good
is to subordinate it to whatever leads to
that choice. And one may not morally do
that, because the basic goods are equally
basic.

But clearly not every inhibition of a
good that occurs as a result of my action
is directly destructive of this good. Some
inhibitions are unsought and unavoidable
side effects of an effort to pursue another
value. Thus one **directly** goes against a
basic good when its inhibition is directly
intended.

When is the destruction of a basic good
directly intended? Here Grisez modifies
the textbook understanding of the double
effect. He believes that the modern formulation is too restrictive. It insists too
much on the behavioral aspect, the physical causality, in determining the meaning
of the act. In the textbook tradition, if
evil is the sole immediate effect of the
physical act, then it is directly produced
and hence directly intended. For example,

one may not "shell out" an ectopic fetus that represents a mortal threat to the mother, though he may excise a pathological tube which contains a fetus. Similarly one may not abort the fetus to save the mother, etc.

Grisez rejects this understanding. Rather he insists that "from the point of view of human moral activity, the initiation of an indivisible process through one's own causality renders all that is involved in that process equally immediate. . . . For on the hypothesis that no other human act intervenes or could intervene, the moral agent who posits a natural cause **simultaneously** (morally speaking) posits its foreseen effects."48

For instance, the saving of the mother is an aspect of the abortifacient act equally immediate, morally speaking, to the death of the child. Thus he writes: "The justification is simply that the very same act, indivisible as to its behavioral process, has both the good effect of protecting human life and the bad effect of destroying it . . . the entire process is indivisible by human choice and hence all aspects of it are equally present to the agent at the moment he makes his choice."49

Central in Grisez's analysis is the indivisibility of the action or behavioral process. It is this indivisibility which allows one to conclude to the equal immediacy of the good and bad effects—and therefore to direct intent of the good and indirect intent of the evil. If, however, the process is divisible and the good effect occurs as a result of a subsequent act, we are dealing with means to end, or with effects not equally immediate. Thus one may not commit adultery to save one's children from a prison camp "because the saving effect would not be present in the adulterous act, but in a subsequent human act—that of the person who releases them." Similarly, organ transplants that will involve deprivation of life or health to the donor are immoral because the two aspects (excision, implant) are factually separable.

Grisez applies this analysis to many instances involving killing. He contends that it is **never** permissible **directly** to take human life. For him, capital punishment cannot be justified. The argument from deterrence, even if factually defensible, is "ethically invalid, because the good is achieved in other human acts, not in the execution itself." Similarly, Grisez argues that killing in warfare is indirect (and must be to remain morally tolerable) much as it is in self-defense.

Thus far Grisez. His ranging analysis of the direct-indirect distinction is by far the most subtle, consistent, and plausible defense of that distinction that I have seen in recent literature. What is to be said of it? First of all, Grisez's notion of an indivisible process seems certainly correct. If the evil effect or aspect occurs within an indivisible process, then "the moral agent who posits a natural cause **simultaneously** (morally speaking) posits its foreseen effects." In other words, the evil effect is not a means, morally speaking, to the good effect. Hence, it is not, or need not be, the object of an intending will. So far so good. What is not clear is why one must be said to turn against a basic good when the evil occurs as a means, and is the object of an intending will. This is the very problem posed by Schüller, as we shall see (below). The problem I am raising centers around the notion of proportionate reason. A closer examination of proportionate reason might have forced Grisez to admit that it need not be ultimately decisive whether the will is intending or permitting, but whether the reason in either case is proportionate. Grisez's reluctance to examine proportionate reason more thoroughly allows him to concentrate his full attention on the posture of the will with reference to the evil in a narrow sense and to frame the problem of unavoidable evil in these terms. If he had discussed what constitutes a proportionate reason more adequately, perhaps we would see a different understanding of what it means to go directly against a basic good.

Behind Grisez's failure to examine more thoroughly the notion of proportionate reason is his deep repugnance to anything resembling a utilitarian calculus. In discussing the four usual conditions for use of the double effect, Grisez says of the last (proportionately grave reason): "The last condition can easily become a field for a

covert, although limited, utilitarianism.
However, that is not necessary. Though
human good is not calculable and though
diverse modes of human good are incommensurable, the basic human goods do
require protection when possible. Human
life may not be destroyed frivolously or
gratuitously . . . where safer methods of
achieving desirable objectives are readily
available."[50]   After this brief statement,
Grisez fairly runs from the notion of proportion and returns to it only to indicate
here and there what reasons are **not** proportionate.   However, the heart of the
matter has been passed over a bit too
quickly here. If one insists—as we should—
that there must be a proportionate reason,
we ask: what is a proportionate reason
for taking another human life?   Or in
Grisez's terms above: what does "when
possible" mean concretely in the phrase
"the basic human goods do require protection when possible?" When is destruction of human life not "frivolous or gra-
tuitous" and why?   We know that lesser
goods such as convenience, avoidance of
shame, health are not to be preferred to

life. But what goods are to be preferred, or at least are of equal status? Grisez does not clarify this because on his own terms he cannot. The basic goods are simply in-commensurable, and to start weighing and balancing them is to succumb to utilitarianism.

haps. But I agree with Stanley Hauerwas that ultimately Grisez cannot "avoid the kind of consequentialist reasoning that our human sensibilities seem to demand in such (conflict) cases."[51]   For if a good like life is simply incommensurable with other goods, what do we mean by a pro-portionate reason where death is, in Grisez's terms, indirect? Proportionate to what? If some goods are to be preferred to life itself, then we have compared life with these goods. And if this is proper, then life can be weighed up against other values too, even very basic values. Grant-ed, there are real dangers and genuine difficulties in a merely utiliterian calculus. But I believe that some such calculus can be avoided only at the·cost of artificiality and contrivance. Our problem is rather to do all we can to guarantee that our calculus will be truly adequate and fully Christian.

Let me put the matter very concretely. In cases (admittedly rare) where abortion is necessary to save the mother's life, Grisez writes: "The justification is simply that the very same act, indivisible as to its behavioral process, has both the good effect of protecting human life and the bad effect of destroying it . . . the entire process is indivisible by human choice and hence all aspects of it are equally present to the agent at the moment he makes his choice."[52]   This is not, in my judgment, the **justification** at all. It is only one way of explaining how the evil that I do is not direct, according to one understanding of what that term means. In other words, this is the justification only on the assumption that an intending will necessarily involves one in turning against a basic good, that is, if directly intended killing is **evil in se**. What is the true justification for allowing abortion here? It cannot be that one may prefer the life of the mother to that of the fetus. For that preference is simply not clear. Furthermore, such a preference gets one into the functional and utilitarian valuations of life that Grisez so rightly abhors. What is the justification—or proportionate reason? Is it not that we are faced here with two alternatives (either abort, or do not abort)? Both alternatives are destructive but one is more destructive than the other. We could allow both mother and child (who will perish under any circumstances) to die; or we could at least salvage one life. Is it not because, **all things considered**, abortion is the lesser evil in this tragic instance? Is it not precisely for this reason, then, that abortion in this instance is proportionate? Is it not for this reason that we may say that the action is truly life–saving? And is it not for this reason that abortion in these circumstances does not involve one in turning against a basic good?

The matter can be urged in another way. Suppose we are faced with a situation (suggested by Philippa Foot) with the following alternatives: an operation which saves the mother but kills the child, versus one that kills the mother but saves the child. In either choice Grisez's use of double effect would seem to apply. That is, there is a single indivisible process one of whose aspects is good, one evil. And the act is life–saving. But unless one uses functional criteria (the "greater value" in some sense of the mother's or child's life) is there a proportionate reason for choosing mother over child, or child over mother? If Grisez would say that in this instance we may save the mother, I ask: why? Why **prefer** the mother to the child when I have a choice? On the other hand, if Grisez says that I may do neither since to do either would involve one in a pre–ference of one life over another, then it seems that what has functioned as pro–portionate reason in instances where he allows abortion to save the mother is this: it is better to save one life than to lose two. Or more generally, a proportionate reason exists because that choice repre–sents the lesser evil.

Frankly, I do not know what Grisez would say to an either–or case of this kind. But I suspect he would hesitate long and hard. But he would not and does not hesitate in the simple instance where abortion (of a fetus who will perish under any circumstances) is necessary to save the mother's life. Does this not indicate that in this latter instance the crucial and decisive consideration is that it is better on all counts in such circumstances to save one life where my only alternative is to lose two? Does it not indicate that the procedure is legitimate precisely for this reason? And does it not then follow that "acting directly against a basic good" need not be interpreted within the deon-tological understanding of direct and in-direct that Grisez provides?

Ultimately, then, Grisez has provided only an ingenious criterion to loosen the notion of direct killing to accommodate the instances where "common sense" seems to allow it. This is a further relaxa-tion of a deontological norm. But it still presupposes that direct killing is evil **in se** and necessarily involves a morally repre-hensible attitude. As I shall indicate later, it can be argued that our moral posture must be measured by a broader intention-ality that relates it to a plurality of values.

In brief, it is the presence or absence of a proportionate reason which determines whether my action—be it direct or indirect psychologically or causally—involves me in turning against a basic good in a way which is morally reprehensible.[53]   Or as Hauerwas puts it: "Grisez does not seem to provide the necessary theoretical account of why so many of our moral arguments take the form of choices between 'lesser evils'."[54]

The most precise and searching challenge to the distinction between direct and indirect voluntary is that of Bruno Schüller.[55]   Schüller notes four areas where the distinction has been used by traditional theology: scandal, cooperation, killing and contraception. But according to Schüller it was used for different reasons where scandal and cooperation are involved. These reasons must be isolated.

The sin of another, Schüller notes, is a moral evil and as such is an absolute disvalue. It would seem to follow that an action (scandal) which has such a disvalue as a foreseen effect must be absolutely avoided. But this would lead to impossible consequences. No lawmaker, for example, could attach a punishment to a violation of law because he would know in advance that this would be the occasion of sinful bribery for a certain undetermined number of people. More fundamentally it is hard to reconcile an absolute duty to avoid foreseen evil with the will of the creator who created a being capable of sin. The way out has always been sought in distinguishing will, intention and purpose from permission and toleration—or direct from indirect. The absolute disvalue of sin demands only that one not will and intend it under any circumstances. However, for a proportionate reason it may be permitted.

The reason the distinction is necessary is that we are dealing here with **moral** evil. The absoluteness of the disvalue forces some such distinction. However, when we are dealing with nonmoral evils (error, pain, sickness, death, etc.) the reason for the distinction between directness and indirectness disappears precisely because these disvalues, fundamental as they are, are **relative** disvalues. These we must, of course, also avoid—but condition-ally. The condition under which we must avoid a relative disvalue is that it does not concur with a greater relative disvalue or an absolute one. For example, sickness must be avoided but not at any price, not, e.g., at the price of plunging one's family into destitution. Schüller argues that when we justifiably cause a relative dis-value in our conduct, we should not call it "indirect." Thus when health officers quarantine one with typhoid fever, should we say that they intend only the preven-tion of its spread and "merely permit" the isolation of the sick individual? Hardly. The isolation is a necessary means to an end. And where means are concerned we speak of an intending will, a direct choice.

We should not abandon this usage. In-deed it brings out the difference between the attitude to moral evil and that to non-moral evil. For a proportionate rea-son we may **permit** a moral evil, but we may directly will and directly cause a nonmoral evil if there is a proportionate reason for doing so.

This has been a tenet of Catholic moral theology for centuries. For instance, one may reveal the hidden defects of another and thereby hurt his reputation "to ward off a relatively important harm from oneself or the neighbor." Similarly with a promise. But this breaking of a promise is experienced by the one to whom the promise was made as an evil. In such cases we do not demand that the negative effect be unintended.

Schüller next turns to killing and contraception. Why did traditional theology feel it necessary to use "direct" and "indirect" when dealing with these subjects? It was because it viewed them as "evil in se." This can be sustained, however, only if the death of a person is an absolute evil in the sense of a moral evil. Once it is granted that the killing of an innocent person is the destruction of a fundamental but nonmoral value, there is no need for the distinction direct-indirect. Rather the assessment is made "teleologically," that is, from presence or absence of proportionate reason.

Schüller concludes, therefore, that death

and contraception must be judged according to teleological, not deontological
norms (these latter being norms independent of proportionate reason). He further
concludes that since this is so, it is superfluous to distinguish between indirect and
direct action. All of them must be judged
according to proportionate reason.

My first reaction to Schüller's analysis
was that it is absolutely correct.[56] After
further reflection, I think that there is
still some unfinished business in it. Here
I should like to raise a question which is
not clearly resolved in his study.

Schüller concludes that the distinction
between direct and indirect is necessary
and functional only where the **sin** of
another (scandal) is concerned. In other
instances the distinction is merely descrip-
tive. This suggests the following problem.
If one says there is a crucial difference
between an intending and a permitting will
where **moral** evil is concerned—as one
must—then that must mean that the will
relates differently to what it intends and
what it permits. Otherwise the distinction
is meaningless and arbitrary. But if the

will relates differently to what it intends
and merely permits in this one instance,
then it must do so wherever that distinction is legitimately made. That is, there
is a different relation to the will when it
intends and merely permits even where
nonmoral evil is concerned. The only
question then is the following: is this
different relationship of moral significance
where **nonmoral** evil is concerned? As I
read him, Schüller says it is not, because
in all instances the action (whether one
intends or merely permits the nonmoral
evil) is to be judged teleologically (that is,
by proportionate reason). However, it can
be doubted that, because both indirect
and direct causing of nonmoral evil are to
be judged teleologically, the same teleological judgment applies to both.

Here something more must be said. Because **direct** (descriptively) killing must
also be judged teleologically, it does not
seem to follow that the same proportionate reason which would justify what is
indirect (descriptively) would always justify what is direct. In other words, there
may be a proportionate reason for doing

something in one way which is not proportionate to doing it another way.

Let us take the death of non-combatants in warfare as an example. Traditional theology has concluded that it can be
permissible (proportionate) at times to
attack the enemy's war machine even
though some non-combatants (innocents)
will be tragically and regretfully killed in
the process. The difficulty of applying
this distinction in practice (that is, determining the non-combatants) does not affect its theoretical legitimacy. It has also
concluded that it is not morally permissible to make these non-combatants the
target of one's attack, to kill them as a
means to bringing the enemy to his knees
and weakening his will to fight. This latter
conclusion is, I believe, a teleological judgment (one based on proportionate reason
defined by forseeable or suspected consequences in the broadest sense), not a
deontological one. Equivalently it means
that direct attacks on non-combatant civilians in wartime, however effective and
important they may seem, will in the long
run release more violence and be more

destructive to human life than the lives we might save by directly attacking non-combatants. But this teleological assessment is concretely different from the teleological assessment made where the deaths are incidental. The difference is not in the number of deaths here and now. They could be numerically the same—for instance, 100 civilians killed incidentally, 100 directly killed. The deaths are equally regrettable and tragic simply as deaths and **in this sense** how they occur does not affect their status as nonmoral evils. But how they occur has a good deal to say about the present meaning of the action, the effect on the agent and others, and hence about the protection and security of life in the long run. These considerations are certainly a part of one's teleological calculus. There are those who argue that it makes little difference to a person whether he is killed by a direct or indirect action, hence that a "love ethic" abandons this distinction. I would urge, contrarily, that it is precisely a "love ethic" which demands the distinction; for a love ethic is concerned not simply with this or that effect, but also with the over-all implications and repercussions of human conduct. And these implications and repercussions are affected very much at times by whether a certain evil is visited by an intending or merely permitting will.

In summary, Schüller's effort has been to show that the norms governing killing and contraception must be built and interpreted teleologically, not deontologically. In this I believe he is correct. But his study leaves the impression that therefore the distinction between direct and indirect is totally superfluous in these areas, and others too. I am not persuaded of this. The nonmoral evil is, to be sure, quantitatively the same whether it is chosen or merely permitted. But the act is not necessarily thereby the same. The relation of the evil to the will, how it happens, not only can tell us what kind of act we are performing, but can have enormously different immediate and long-term implications, and therefore generate a quite different calculus of proportion. I am suggesting, therefore, that the terms direct-indirect are not superfluous, or at least

not at all times, but only that a different
teleological calculus may apply in each
instance.

This problem can be restated in terms
of Schüller's analysis of cooperation in
another's evil doing. Schüller argues that
the distinction between direct and indirect
is not necessary here. For whether one
performs or refuses the cooperation has
no influence on the **moral** violation of the
other, but only on the effects of this
moral violation. Schüller takes the example of a bank-cashier during a robbery.
The cashier may and should hand over the
money not because this leaves the robber
less morally guilty, but because the loss of
money is a lesser nonmoral evil than loss
of life. The moral guilt of the robber is in
his determination to kill during the robbery if necessary. The cashier, Schüller
notes, cannot lessen this. But he can
lessen the nonmoral disvalues that the
robber is prepared to commit. In this
instance the cashier can **intend** to cause
the harm to the bank to save his own life.
There is, says Schüller, no need to appeal
to indirectness here. The problem is anal-

yzed teleologically.

I agree with this analysis, but I believe that something more must be said. Schüller says the cashier should hand over the money because the loss of money is a lesser nonmoral evil than loss of life. That is certainly true. But must we not add also that preserving one's life in this way will in the long run threaten more lives and undermine the very value I am protecting in this instance? Let us return to the case of the rioting mob and the judge. In Schüller's analysis we would have to say that the **moral** guilt of the mob is already there in its determination to kill five men unjustly if the judge does not frame one innocent man and execute him. Therefore this moral evil cannot be lessened. But the judge can lessen the nonmoral disvalues the mob is prepared to commit by executing one innocent man. Certainly the death of one innocent man is a lesser evil than the death of five innocent men. Schüller (if his analysis stops where it does) would be forced to conclude that the judge should execute the one innocent man. Yet I think we are appalled at this

conclusion. Is it not precisely because we
sense that taking the life of this innocent
man in these circumstances would represent a capitulation to and encouragement
of a type of injustice which in the long
run would render many more lives vulnerable? Yet our judgment would be different if the death of the one innocent
man were incidental. In summary, proportion must be measured also in terms
of long-term effects. And in terms of
such effects, whether one directly intends
(or not) certain nonmoral evils he now
does may make quite a difference.

In other words, the teleological character of all our norms does not eliminate
the relevance of the distinction between
direct-indirect where nonmoral values and
disvalues are involved. Rather precisely
because these norms are teleological is the
direct-indirect distinction relevant. For
the relation of the evil-as-it-happens to
the will may say a great deal about the
meaning of my action, its repercussions
and implications, and therefore what will
happen to the good in question over the
long haul. If one asks why, I believe the

answer is to be found in the fact that an intending will represents a closer relation of the agent to the disvalue and therefore indicates a greater willingness that the disvalue occur.

These are some of the recent attempts to deal with conflict situations in a sinful and imperfect world. All of these studies make valid and necessary points and I have found all of them illuminating. If a single thread or theme is common to all of them, it is, as Charles Curran has pointed out, this: dissatisfaction with the narrowly behavioral or physical understanding of human activity that underlies the standard interpretation of direct and indirect. I agree with this dissatisfaction. On the other hand, in making their points they all seem in one way or another incomplete, and even misleading when dealing with the distinction between direct and indirect intention.

For instance Knauer rightly rejects the use of "moral evil" to describe actions independently of the reasons for which they are done, hence independently of their context and intention. However, in interpreting the direct–indirect distinction in an exclusively moral way (that is, with no relation to psychological intentionality), he underestimates the real differences in the meaning of our conduct that could be generated by psychological intentionality. Grisez provides a satisfying account of the origin of moral obligation with his analysis of basic human goods. But his interpretation of what it means "to turn directly against these goods" seems too contrived and incapable of accounting for the complexity of reality, especially of the conflict situations we have been considering. This is traceable to his reluctance to examine more realistically the notion of proportionate reason, a reluctance rooted in his nervous fear of any utilitarian calculus.

Van der Marck and Van der Poel rightly insist that the meaning of our actions must take account of intersubjectivity (Van der Marck) and intentionality (Van der Poel). However, both authors seem too readily to accept the idea that once an action is described in terms of its dominant intentionality (e.g., "removing the effects of rape") it has been justified, or that the only calculus which is of any help in weighing the moral quality of the decision is community-building or destroying.

Schüller is certainly correct in his insistence on the difference between moral and nonmoral evil and therefore on the profound difference between actions occasioning the sin of another and actions visiting nonmoral disvalues on the neighbor. Similarly, I believe he is correct in insisting that the meaning of moral norms concerning nonmoral evils must be interpreted within the confines of a teleological calculus (as long as a greater evil would not result, etc.) However, his preoccupation with this point leads him to suggest that direct and indirect intention are altogether morally irrelevant where nonmoral evil is associated with our activity. This fails to take seriously enough the real contribution of intentionality to the significance of human actions. In doing so it could leave him somewhat vulnerable to the weaknesses of a merely numerical calculus of proportionality.

In conclusion I should like to attempt

a synthesis that takes advantage of the above positions but seems identifiable with no one of them. Such a critical synthesis will remain incomplete, and even vulnerable, I am sure. Not only does the problem we are dealing with involve one's whole moral theory (an area where there is considerably less clarity and certainty than is desirable), but it also brings this theory to bear on practical day-to-day problems. One is asked to be both theoretically consistent and practically sensitive to the complexity and intransigence of reality—in other words, to plug all the loopholes in a prudent and persuasive way. This is particularly difficult in times where theologians have different views on how the loopholes ought to be plugged, if they should be plugged at all! The following reflections must, therefore, remain a thought-experiment and will represent above all a useful invitation to other theologians to correct the shortcomings, inconsistencies, and even errors they may contain. My own very tentative conclusions would be summarized in the following statements:

1. There is a difference between an intending and permitting will, and therefore in the human action involving the one or the other.

2. In a conflict situation, the relation of the evil to the value sought is partially determinative of the posture of the will (whether intending or permitting).

3. The basic structure, however, in conflict situations is avoidable-unavoidable evil, the principle of the lesser evil.

4. Both the intending and the permitting will (where evil is involved) are to be judged teleologically (that is, by presence or absence of proportionate reason).

5. Proportionate reason means three things: (a) a value at stake at least equal to that sacrificed; (b) no other way of salvaging it here and now; (c) its protection here and now will not undermine it in the long run.

6. The notion of proportionate reason is analogous.

An explanation of each of these will provide the context for my own modified understanding of the moral relevance of the direct-indirect distinction.

1. There is a difference between an intending and a permitting will.

If the distinction between an intending and permitting will is utterly essential and profoundly meaningful where the moral evil (sin) of another is concerned, as Schüller rightly maintains, that can mean but one thing: there is a real difference between an intending and permitting will. Otherwise we are dealing with mere words, as was pointed out above. Now if there is a real difference between an intending and permitting will, then this difference must show where nonmoral evil is concerned. That in turn means that the human action involving an intending will (of evil) is or at least can be, a different human action from that involving a permitting will. To say anything else is to say that intentionality does not affect the meaning of human activity, a tenet that becomes inconsistent if one reverses it where **sin** is concerned. This difference between an intending and permitting will generates two important conclusions, one negative, one positive. First of all, it is not simply and exclusively the existence

or non-existence of an evil effect that
determines the meaning of the action that
occasioned it. How this evil relates to the
human will is also relevant. A love ethic
is, indeed, concerned with effects; but it
must also be concerned with how they
occur. Why? Because secondly, actions
which are different because of differing
intentionality have a different immediate
meaning and may lead to different social
and long-term effects.

To admit that there is a difference between an intending and permitting will
within an action is not to deny that the
overall significance of the action is affected by intention of the end, a point clearly
made by Van der Marck and Van der Poel.
Nor is it to deny a certain unity of the
action rooted in this intentionality. It is
simply to say that within such ultimate
purposefulness the will can assume at
least two different postures vis-à-vis the
evil that is associated with one's choice.
That this difference can be morally significant is suggested by the instance of the
intention or permission of the sin of
another. How should this difference be

explained? The matter remains somewhat
mysterious, as Schüller notes. But we can
say this much at least: the intending will
(hence the person) is more closely associated with the existence of evil than the
merely permitting will. Furthermore I
believe we must say that an intending will
is more willing that the evil be than is a
permitting will. That this can have morally significant repercussions I shall attempt
to indicate later.

2. **In a conflict situation, the relation
of the evil caused to the value sought is
partially**[57]   **determinative of the posture
of the will (whether intending or permitting).** It seems that nonmoral evil can be
immediately associated with human activity in at least two distinguishable ways:
as an aspect of the act with no casual
relation to the good effect; as means with
a necessary causal relationship to the good
envisaged. That which stands in a relationship of means to end is necessarily the
object of an intending will, even if not
propter se. That which is merely effect or
aspect need not be. When is the evil in a
causal relationship to the good, a means

to it, and therefore necessarily the object of an intending will? I would be willing to accept Grisez's criterion: if the evil occurs within an indivisible process, then in the moral sense it is equally immediate with the good effect, and hence not a means. If, however, the process is divisible so that the good effect occurs as the result of a subsequent act, we are clearly dealing with a means, and an intending will. There are difficulties in this criterion because it moves a step away from our psychological experience of permission. Concretely, it is much clearer that we are dealing with a means when there is divisibility than it is that we are not when the process is indivisible. For some evils that are part of an indivisible process do seem to be means. Be that as it may, Grisez's criterion can be accepted provisionally.

An example will bring out the difference between the intending and permitting will. If a woman has cancer of the ovaries, a bilateral oophorectomy is performed. The result: sterility. If a family has seven children, the wife is weak, the husband is out of a job, the woman may have her tubes tied on the occasion of the last delivery. The result: sterility. The immediate effect (nonmoral evil) is the same in both cases, sterility. Obviously these actions are different human actions in terms of their overall intentionality—the good sought. One is a life-saving intervention, the other a family-saving or family-stabilizing act, so to speak. But even within this larger difference, the bearing of the will toward the sterility is, I believe, distinguishable in the two instances. For the moment no moral relevance will be assigned to this difference. But it seems that there is a difference and the difference originates in the relation of the nonmoral evil to the good sought. In the one instance, the nonmoral evil is chosen as a means; in the other it is not. Van der Marck and Van der Poel have been reluctant to admit the category of means in this regard. But one need not unduly fragment the wholeness or unity of the overall action to allow the validity of this distinction within it.

Because the forms of associated evil are distinguishable within our actions, the psychological experience of "intention" is somewhat different in each case. General reluctance that the evil must be brought about (whether "intended" or "permitted") is presumably common to both instances. Still when the evil is an effect or aspect with no necessary causal relationship to the good being pursued, one does indeed have a different psychological awareness of the evil involved than he does when there is a necessary causal relationship between the evil and good achieved. I have suggested that this psychological difference is traceable to the fact that an intending will is more closely associated with the evil, more "willing" that the evil exist. The crucial question is whether (and why) this single form of psychological awareness—that associated with evil as aspect—is normative for a proper human intentionality. The traditional answer has been "yes," at least in the instances involving human life and our sexual faculties. That is, the evil involved must be unintended **in that one psychological sense**. I believe that there are good reasons to doubt this conclusion and to

assert that the meaning of human intentionality toward nonmoral evil is to be
determined by reference to a larger can-
vas.

3. **The basic analytic structure in conflict situations is the lesser evil, or morally
avoidable–unavoidable evil.** The rule of
double effect is a vehicle for dealing with
conflict situations. When we see the
situations it was trying to meet, we can
discern its essential elements. It was
facing conflict situations where only two
courses are available: to act or not to act,
to speak or remain silent, to resist or not
to resist. The concomitant of either
course of action was harm of some sort.
Now in situations of this kind, the rule of
Christian reason, if we are governed by
the **ordo bonorum**, is to choose the lesser
evil. This general statement is, it would
seem, beyond debate; for the only alternative is that in conflict situations we
should choose the greater evil, which is
patently absurd. This means that all concrete rules and distinctions are subsidiary
to this and hence valid to the extent that
they actually convey to us what is factual-

ly the lesser evil. This is true of the distinction between direct and indirect voluntariety. It is a vehicle, not a principle—and a vehicle as useful as its accuracy in mediating and concretizing the more general principle. Now, if in a conflict situation one does what is, in balanced Christian judgment (and in this sense "objectively"), the lesser evil, his intentionality must be said to be integral. It is in this larger sense that I would attempt to read Thomas' statement that moral acts **"recipiunt speciem secundum id quod intenditur."**[58]   Thus the basic category for conflict situations is the lesser evil, or avoidable–unavoidable evil, or proportionate reason.

Because the evil caused was so often genuinely incidental and associated with a permitting will (psychologically), the distinction between direct and indirect came to be identified with proper intentionality. That is, from being a subordinate vehicle in service of the determination of the lesser evil, it became a principle of this determination. Awareness of its broad rootage gave way to a concentration on

the actions, their causality and the psychological posture of the will in explaining the idea of twofold effect. Actually,
where nonmoral evil is concerned, direct
voluntariety says but one thing: the evil
has a causal relation to the good and is
willed as a means. This becomes morally
decisive only when the posture of the will
affects the determination of what is, all
things considered, the lesser or greater
evil.

I am arguing, therefore, that the essential ingredients that led to the formulation
of the rule of double effect are two: (1)
the legitimacy, desirability, or above all
necessity of a certain good (self-defense,
saving the mother, resisting national aggression, rescuing another, etc.); (2) the
inseparability of this good from harm or
evil in the circumstances. But evil-as-
effect (or aspect) of the action is only one
form of this inseparability of evil from a
desirable good. Another form is evil-as-
means.

Concretely, it can be argued that where
a higher good is at stake and the only
means to protect it is to choose to do a

nonmoral evil, then the will remains properly disposed to the values constitutive of human good (Grisez's "basic goods," Schüller's **ordo bonorum**), that the person's attitude or intentionality is good because he is making the best of a destructive and tragic situation. This is to say that the intentionality is good even when the person, reluctantly and regretfully to be sure, intends the nonmoral evil if a truly proportionate reason for such a choice is present.

To face conflict situations exclusively in terms of a psychological understanding of the terms "direct" and "indirect" could be to give a narrow and restrictive reading to the overall intent of St. Thomas. Be that as it may, we know that later theologians moved away from this analysis of self-defense and stated that some conflict situations could legitimately involve one in intending (reluctantly) nonmoral evil as a means. For instance, M. Zalba, S.J., in his treatment of capital punishment, defends the **direct** killing of criminals by appeal to the common good: "Without it (capital punishment) the public common

good cannot survive, if one considers the
malice and daring of criminals. . . ."
The factual validity of this argument can
be denied; but what is important here is
the theoretical structure of the argument.
Zalba, with many other theologians, is
arguing that there are greater goods than
an individual human life and when they
are threatened and there is no other way
to circumvent this threat, then it is reasonable to choose to do the evil to achieve
the good, or avoid the evil.

Similarly Zalba (with many others)
holds that in situations of self-defense
against unjust aggression one may legitimately intend the wounding or death of
the assailant as "a legitimate and upright
means instituted by God for the prose-
cution of one's right. . . ."[60] The appeal
to the double effect, he says, appears
"obscurior" precisely because "the preservation of one's own life is achieved
through the wounding of another life
rather than as a concomitant of this
wounding." Once again, the structure of
the argument is similar: one may intend
nonmoral evil as a means if it is the only

way of protecting a good judged to be at least proportionate.

There are other instances where we see a similar teleological model operative. One may legitimately intend the deception of another through falsehood to preserve a professional secret. To say that the deception is indirect and unintended (psychologically) as Zalba does, is unnecessary—and, in his case, inconsistent if he argues as he does where self–defense and capital punishment are concerned. Why did he not argue that deliberate, intended deception of another is a legitimate means to a proportionately grave good otherwise unobtainable? In the recent past theologians argued (correctly in my view) that women could directly sterilize themselves against the very real possibility of pregnancy–by–rape.[61] Once again, what is this but an avowal that I may reasonably choose to do nonmoral evil (as a means) if it is justified by a truly proportionate reason?

These reflections suggest that the moral integrity of one's intentionality cannot be restrictively defined in terms of the psychological indirectness associated with evil–as–an–effect (or aspect) of an indivisible process even where the basic goods are concerned. Psychologically unintended evil effects are but an example of legitimate intentionality. But if the unintended effect is but one example of integral intentionality, and if intended means can be another, then it seems clear that integral intentionality traces not to psychological indirectness as such when evil occurs, but exclusively to the proportionate reason for acting. If there is a truly proportionate reason for acting, the agent remains properly open and disposed toward the **ordo bonorum** whether the evil occurs as an indivisible effect or as a means within the action. However, since evil–as–means and evil–as–effect are different realities, they may demand different proportionate reasons. What is sufficient for **allowing** an evil may not in all cases be sufficient for **choosing** it as a means.

4. Both the intending and permitting will are to be judged teleologically (that is, by presence or absence of proportion–

ate reason). Even though there is a real difference between an intending and permitting will, and hence a real difference between actions involving the one or other, the moral relevance of this distinction must be approached delicately. In the past it was too readily concluded that if an evil occurred in conjunction with an intending will it was thereby immoral. This was especially true where the values of life and sexuality were concerned. The present reaction against this is a statement to the effect that it is simply the existence of the evil, not its relation to the intending or permitting will which has moral significance. Both positions are, I believe, one-sided, and, if urged, extreme. The mediating position suggested here is that there is a difference between an intending and permitting will where concomitant premoral evil is concerned, but that both must be judged teleologically.

Concretely, the supposition behind the assertion that certain evils are morally tolerable only if they are indirect with regard to human intentionality is either one of the following two: (1) there are no higher values; (2) or if there are, they are never in conflict with lesser values. For if there are higher values and if they will be lost or threatened unless one sacrifices the lesser values, and if this choice will not subvert the relevant values in the long run, then what is wrong with choosing, reluctantly to be sure, to do the nonmoral evil that the greater good may be achieved? Is there a reasonable, defensible alternative to this? If there is, I do not see it. This leads to the conclusion that in those instances where nonmoral evil has been viewed as justified because it is indirect, the psychological indirectness was not radically decisive at all. What was and is decisive is the proportionate reason for acting. Similarly, in those instances that have been traditionally viewed as immoral because the intentionality was direct, the psychological directness itself is not decisive. The immorality must be argued from lack of proportionate reason. An example of each instance will clarify the point of the argument.

In discussing indirect sterilization, Edwin Healy, S.J. presents the following case:

"The patient has had many vaginal deliveries and as a result lacerations, infections, and erosions have occurred in the **cervix uteri**. Moreover, there has been subinvolution of the uterus and the organ itself has become heavy, boggy, enlarged and weakened, and is now causing the patient great physical debility, pain and distress. May the physician excise the uterus for the present relief of the patient?"[62] The operation will, of course, result in sterilization—an evil effect, a disvalue when viewed abstractly. Healy approves the operation as a justified **indirect** sterilization, for "the condition described above would be sufficiently grave to justify this operation if less radical treatment would not prove effective." Is this not simply at root a calculus which asserts that the pain, debility and distress caused by the uterus are greater disvalues than the loss of fertility entailed in its removal—and that sacrificing fertility in this instance will not subvert its value in the long run? "Indirect" here means one thing: the sterility is not chosen as a means. The term should not imply that one may never choose infertility as a means.

The principle of discrimination in the conduct of war (non–combatant immunity) may serve as the second instance. This principle has traditionally been presented as a moral absolute, and the direct killing of innocent persons viewed as intrinsically evil, evil in se. That is, such killing is morally evil regardless of the circumstances and independently of the consequences. Here I should like tó suggest that it is precisely because of foreseen consequences that such a principle is a practical absolute. In this perspective its meaning would be: even though certain short–term advantages might be gained by taking innocent life in warfare, ultimately and in the long run, the harm would far outweigh the good. Taking innocent human life as a means to (e.g.) demoralizing the enemy, totalizes warfare. The action is radically different in human terms from the incidental death of innocents as one attempts to repel the enemy's war machine, even though the evil effects are numerically the same. It is radically different basically

because of the intentionality involved, and
to deny to intentionality any realistic
place in determining the meaning of human choice. Taking innocent human life
as a means removes restraints and unleash-
es destructive powers which both now and
in the long run will brutalize sensitivities
and take many more lives than we would
now save by such action. We cannot
prove this type of assertion with a syllo-
gistic click, but it is a good human bet
given our knowledge of ourselves and our
history—at least good enough to generate
a practically exceptionless imperative, the
type of moral rule Donald Evans refers to
as "virtually exceptionless."[63]

What is responsible for this difference?
This is the crucial question, of course, and
one that cannot be answered (or at least
has not been) with full satisfaction. Above
it was suggested that the intending will
(hence the person) is more closely associated with the evil than is a permitting will.
This bespeaks (in some admittedly obscure
way) a greater willingness that it occur.
Now such a willingness is morally acceptable only to the extent that such an

intention represents a choice of what is
the lesser evil.

This analysis is not without its weaknesses. Suppose, for instance, two situations where one and the same good could
be realized. In the first situation it can be
realized only by intending the evil; in the
second it can be realized by permitting the
evil. If someone is ready to bring the
good into existence only by permitting
the evil, it has been suggested that he is
less willing that the evil exist. Yet it must
be said that he is also less willing that the
good exist. Furthermore, the person who
is prepared to realize the good even by intending the evil is more willing that the
evil exist, but only because he is more
willing that the good exist. Ultimately,
therefore, to say that the intending will
is more closely associated with evil than
a merely permitting will is somewhat cir-
cular and considerably less than satisfying.

Joseph L. Allen views the principle of
non-combatant immunity from direct attack as one generated teleologically, by a
consideration of consequences. Of this
principle he states: "Such limits represent

the fact that in the overwhelming number of cases, the strategist will be far more destructive by transgressing the rule than by following it."[64]   Therefore the rule of non–combatant immunity is a virtually exceptionless moral principle not independently of a calculation of consequences, but precisely because of an adequate calculation. Thus Allen writes: "Calculation over whether to obliterate a city is too narrow if it asks only whether this action would 'shorten the war' or assist in the attaining of military objectives.   The strategist must also consider several other possible effects of the proposed action, if he is actually concerned for the total result: the destruction of people who have little direct relation to the war effort; the destruction of the social fabric of the city and its surrounding area; the invitation the raid gives, both to the opponent and to one's own side, to conduct more and more attacks of this sort, perhaps out of revenge and often out of all proportion to some 'better peace'; and the increased callousness to creaturely beings that tends to accompany such acts.

. . .The effect of an act on the whole range
of creaturely beings must be considered,
not merely its effect on a narrowly con-
ceived military goal."[65]

What Allen is saying is that killing
innocent people **as a means** in warfare is
wrong because there is no proportionate
reason for doing this, if our calculation of
proportionality is adequate. This leads
him to conclude that the end does not
justify the means, but that the **ends** do.
That is, before an adequate moral assessment of an act can be made, its effect on
all the ends or values must be weighed. In
the case of indiscriminate warfare, our
experience and reflection tell us that all
the ends or values will not be best served
by such actions. Or, as Charles Curran
puts it, "all of the moral values must be
considered and a final decision made after
all the moral values have been compared."[66]   It is this weighing of all the
moral values that has made of non-combatant immunity a virtually exceptionless
moral rule. Proportionality is always the
criterion where our actions cause damage.
Our major problem is to make sure that

we do not conceive it narrowly. The strength of our moral norms touching concrete conduct is an elaboration of what we judge, within our culture, with our history and experience, to be proportionate or disproportionate.

If there are norms that are teleologically established and yet are "virtually exceptionless"—as I believe there are—the remaining theological task is to clarify those metaethical assertions in view of which these norms are held as exceptionless. Above I referred to the fact that "we sense that taking the life of this innocent man in these circumstances would . . . in the long run render many more lives vulnerable." Of the direct destruction of non-combatants in warfare I have said that it would "in the long run . . . take many more lives than we would now save by such action." These are non-demonstrable calculations, prudential judgments based on both the certainties of history and the uncertainties of the future. Our sense of what we ought to do and ought not to do is informed by our past experience and a certain agnosticism with regard to our future behavior and its long-term effects. This leads to the suggestion—and it is only that—that where we view norms as "virtually exceptionless," we do so or ought to do so because of the prudential validity of what we refer to technically as **lex lata in praesumptione periculi communis** (a law established on the presumption of common and universal danger).

The notion of a presumption of universal danger is one most frequently associated with positive law. Its sense is that even if the action in question does not threaten the individual personally, there remains the further presumption that to allow individuals to make that decision for themselves will pose a threat for the common good. For instance, in time of drought, all outside fires are sometimes forbidden. This prohibition of outside fires is founded on the presumption that the threat to the common welfare cannot be sufficiently averted if private citizens are allowed to decide for themselves what precautions are adequate.

It seems to me that the exceptionless character of the norm prohibiting direct killing of non-combatants in warfare might be argued in a way analogous to this. The risk in alternative policies is simply too great. There are enormous goods at stake, and both our past experience of human failure, inconstancy, and frailty, and our uncertainty with regard to long-term effects lead us to believe that we **ought** to hold some norms as virtually exceptionless, that this is the conclusion of prudence in the face of dangers too momentous to make risk tolerable.

5. **Proportionate reason means three things**: (a) a value at least equal to that sacrificed is at stake; (b) there is no less harmful way of protecting the value here and now; (c) the manner of its protection here and now will not undermine it in the long run. If one examines carefully all instances where the occurrence of evil is judged acceptable in human action, a single decisive element is at the heart of the analysis: proportionate reason as here described. Under scrutiny this term must include the three elements mentioned. This understanding of proportionality is very close to that of Knauer. However, he

maintains that when the reason is proportionate in the sense stated, the evil caused or permitted is indirect. I would prefer to say that the evil is direct or indirect depending on the basic posture of the will, but that it is justified in either case if a genuinely proportionate reason (in the sense stated) is present. The position suggested here is an attempt to incorporate into our moral reasoning all aspects of proportionality, immediate and long term, in contrast to a position that would appeal exclusively to the criterion of "community-building," or rely too narrowly on psychological directness and indirectness as decisive without further ado.

The foregoing could be put negatively as follows. An action is disproportionate in any of the following instances: if a lesser value is preferred to a more important one; if evil is unnecessarily caused in the protection of a greater good; if, in the circumstances, the manner of protecting the good will undermine it in the long run.

It is with reference to this third aspect of proportionality that the difference between an intending and permitting will (direct and indirect) reveals its potential moral relevance. Thus where nonmoral evil is involved, even if the good at stake is quantitatively proportionate to or greater than the loss, protecting it **in this way** could in the long run undermine this good. The principle of non-combatant immunity would seem to be an example of this.

The judgment of proportionality in conflict situations is not only a very decisive judgment; it is also a most difficult one. To see whether an action involving evil is proportionate in the circumstances we must judge whether this choice is the best possible service of all the values in the tragic and difficult conflict. What is the best possible promotion of all the values in the circumstances will depend on how one defines "in the circumstances." A truly adequate account of the circumstances will read them to mean not just how much **quantitative** good can be salvaged from an individual conflict of values, but it will also weigh the social implications and reverberating after-effects in so far as they can be foreseen.

It will put the choice to the test of
generalizability ("What if all men in similar circumstances were to act in this
way?"). It will consider the cultural
climate, especially in terms of the biases
and reactions it is likely to favor in a one-
sided way. It will draw whatever wisdom
it can from past experience and reflection,
particularly as embodied in the rules men
of the past have found a useful guide in
difficult times. It will seek the guidance
of others whose maturity, experience, reflection and distance from the situation
offer a counterbalance to the self-interest-
ed tendencies we all experience. It will
allow the full force of one's own religious
faith and its intentionalities to interpret
the meaning and enlighten the options of
the situation. This is what an adequate
and responsible account of the circumstances must mean. So informed, an
individual is doing the best he can and all
that can be expected of him. But to say
these things is to say that an individual
will depend on communal discernment
much more than our contemporary indivi-
dualistic attitudes suggest.

6. **The notion of proportionate reason is analogous.** The comments made above (n. 5) should not lead us to believe that the concept of proportionate reason is reducible to a simple utilitarian calculus. Far from it. The notion is much more difficult than traditional casuistry would lead us to believe and, I believe, somewhat more fruitful and Christian than deontologists would allow us to imagine. Perhaps the problem can be introduced by a concrete instance. Moral theologians have judged as heroic charity the choice of a soldier to throw himself (at the cost of his own life) on a live explosive to save the life of a fellow soldier or soldiers. This means that they have asserted that, in technical terms, there is a proportionate reason for doing this. On the other hand, they have also asserted that an individual is not obliged to do this. In other words, there is a proportionate reason also for not making such a choice.

Somewhat similarly, if one has a proportionate reason for throwing himself on an explosive to save the life of his friend, then he also has a proportionate reason for allowing an assailant to kill him in preference to defending himself. Indeed, an unjust assailant is in a legitimate sense, precisely in his injustice, one's neighbor in greatest need. What then does proportionate reason mean if it can yield either conclusion?

The criterion of proportionality is that **ordo bonorum** viewed in Christian perspective, for it is the **ordo bonorum** which is determinative of the good one should attempt to do and the criterion of the objectively loving character of one's activity. In the light of this **ordo bonorum** there are three distinct possible and general senses of "proportionate reason."

First, there is the situation where the only alternative to causing or permitting evil is greater evil. This is the instance where both mother and fetus will certainly die without an abortion but where at least the mother can be saved with an abortion. It is also the case of the drowning swimmer where the hopeful rescuer cannot be of help because he cannot swim. The mother cannot save the child; under no condition can she do him any good. Similarly the bystander cannot save the drowning man. He can do him no good. It would be immoral to try. One who cannot save another but still tries is no longer governed by the **ordo bonorum**. For love (as involving, besides **benevolentia**, also **beneficentia**) is always controlled by the possible. There is no genuine **beneficentia** if no good can accrue to the individual through my sacrifice. An act of love (as **beneficentia**) is not measured by the mere desire or intention (**benevolentia**). Therefore, in instances like this, abortion and not attempting to save the drowning swimmer are proportionately grounded decisions precisely because the harm cannot be avoided, whereas harm to the mother and prospective rescuer can and should be avoided. Into this first category of proportionality would fall also the standard cases where falsehood is uttered as the necessary means to protect a patient's confidence and reputation, etc.

Secondly, proportionate reason in a different sense is realized in situations where the alternatives are not so obvious. This is the instance where I lay down my

life for another (or others). In this instance a good equal to what I sacrifice
accrues to another and is the only way of
securing that good for him. This is proportionate not because his life is prefer-
able to mine—they are equally valuable as
basic human goods—but because in case
of conflict, it is a human and Christian
good to seek to secure this good for my
neighbor even at the cost of my life. Indeed, other things being equal, such self-
sacrifice is the ultimate act of human love.
It is an assertion-in-action that "greater
love than this no man has than that he lay
down his life for his friends." To deny
that such sacrifice could be proportionately grounded would be to deny that
self-giving love after the model of Christ
is a human good and represents the direc-
tion in which we should all be growing.

By saying that self-sacrifice to save the
neighbor can truly be proportionate, traditional theology has implied that the goods
being weighed, the alternatives are not
simply physical human life, my life vs.
that of another. Rather it has implied:
(a) a world in which conflict occurs; (b) a

world in which we are not mature in charity; (c) that the most maturing choices in
such a world of conflict and sin are, other
things being equal, those which prefer the
good of others to self after the example
of Christ. Preference of another to self is
only thinkable as a good in a world both
objectively and **subjectively** infected by
sin and weakness: "objectively" in terms
of conflict situations where death and
deprivation are tragic possibilities that
cannot be prevented except by corre-
sponding or greater loss; "subjectively" in
terms of the fact that being immature in
grace and love, we tend to view such situations in terms of our own personal good
exclusively and primarily—whereas our
growth and perfection as human beings
are defined in terms of our being, like the
Triune God himself, **ad alterum**, a being
for others.

Thirdly, some actions or omissions were
said to be proportionately grounded because the preference of a good for or in
another at the cost of that good in or for
myself should not, in view of human
weakness and immaturity, be demanded.

To say anything else would be to impose
perfect love on imperfect creatures under
pain of separation from divine friendship.
This would be disproportionate because it
would crush human beings and turn them
from God. We know that the manuals of
moral theology were often designed with
confessional practice in mind. This means
that casuistry was often concerned with
what is sinful to do or omit rather than
whether it was Christianly good to aspire
to a particular value. Is it not to be expected that this perspective would also
appear at the level of "proportionate reason"? Understandably, therefore, scholas-
tic tradition has always maintained the
axiom: **"Caritas non obligat cum gravi in-
commodo."** In other words, there is a
proportionate reason for not aiding my
neighbor in his distress or need. This
axiom must be carefully understood if
this third sense of proportionate reason is
not to compromise genuine Christianity.

Could we approach it as follows? It is
important, first of all, to admit that the
allegation that Christ knew nothing of
"excusing causes," "extraordinary mea-

sures," "excessive inconvenience," etc. where fraternal love was involved is assuredly correct. However, Christ was proclaiming an ideal after which we should strive and which we will realize perfectly only after this life and the purgations preparatory to eternal life. "Love one another as I have loved you" is a magnificent ideal. Our growth and maturity depend on our continued pursuit of it. But nobody has ever achieved it. This disparity between ideal and achievement suggests an explanation of the maxim under discussion which will show that it is not incompatible with, but even demanded by, the gospel message. That is, it suggests the imperfection of our charity in this life.

What I have in mind is something like this. To propose a deep knowledge of the physical science as desirable, as an ideal, is one thing. To demand of a ten-year-old that he master the subtleties of atomic physics under pain of deprivation of further instruction probably means that I will put an end to the individual's whole educational process. To propose bodily health as an ideal is proper and necessary. To demand that a tubercular patient recover his health all at once under pain of relapse into serious illness means that he is condemned to ill health. Similarly, to propose the Savior's love as an ideal is helpful and necessary. But to demand of mens' charity the perfection of virtue exemplified and preached by Jesus under pain of deprivation of charity itself (mortal sin) would be to condemn men to life in mortal sin. This can hardly be thought to be the message of One who knew men so thoroughly that he came to redeem them. Hence, when one asserts limits to charity, he is not emasculating the gospel message; he is rather asserting it, but insisting that it was proclaimed to imperfect men who must grow to its fullness. One dare not forget this. For if charity can be minimalized out of existence, it can also be maximalized out of existence. When proclamation and immediate demand are confused, the proclamation can easily be lost in the impossibility of the demand.

The adage we are dealing with, therefore, simply recognizes human limits and the consequent imperfection of our chari-

ty. It is saying that we do not lose divine
life for failing to have and express its fullness now. The ideal remains. It is there—
to be sought, pursued, struggled after.
But it is precisely because its achievement
demands constant pursuit that it would be
inconsistent with the charity of the gospel
message to assert that its demands exceed
the limitations of the human pursuer.
This is the third sense of "proportionate
reason."

This study would very tentatively conclude, therefore, that the traditional distinction between direct and indirect is
neither as exclusively decisive as we pre-
viously thought, nor as widely dispensable
as some recent studies suggest. As des-
criptive of the posture of the will toward
a particular evil (whether intending or
permitting), it only aids us in understanding what we are doing. Whether the action
so described represents integral intentionality more generally and overall depends
on whether it is, or is not, **all things considered**, the lesser evil in the circumstances.
This is an assessment that cannot be col-
lapsed into a mere determination of direct

and indirect voluntariety. Hence the
traditional distinction, while morally relevant, cannot be the basis for deontologically exceptionless norms—which is not to
say that there are no virtually exceptionless norms. Quite the contrary in my
judgment.

This conclusion will no doubt appear
rationally somewhat untidy. But it is, I
believe, a reflection of the gap that exists
between our moral sensitivities and judgments, and our ability to systematize them
rationally. Moral awareness and judgments
are fuller and deeper than "rational arguments" and rational categories. They are
the result of evidence in the broadest
sense—which includes a good deal more
than mere rational analysis. While moral
judgments must continually be submitted
to rational scrutiny in an effort to correct
and nuance them, in the last analysis,
rooting as they do in the intransigence
and complexity of reality, they remain
deeper and more obscure than the systems
and arguments we devise to make them
explicit.[67]

1. Cf. Joseph T. Mangan, S.J., "An Historical Analysis of the Principle of Double Effect," *Theological Studies,* 10 (1949), 40–61; J. Ghoos, "L'Acte à double effet: Étude de Théologie Positive," *Ephemerides Theologicae Lovanienses,* 27 (1951), 30–52.

2. Cf. for example, G. Kelly, S.J., *Medico-Moral Problems* (St. Louis: Catholic Hospital Association, 1958), pp. 13ff.; G. Grisez, *Abortion: The Myths. the Realities, and the Arguments* (Washington: Corpus Books, 1970), p. 329.

3. Paul Ramsey, *The Just War* (New York: Scribners, 1968), and especially *War and the Christian Conscience* (Durham: Duke University Press, 1961).

4. John C. Ford, S.J., "The Morality of Obliteration Bombing," *Theological Studies,* 5 (1944), 261–309.

5. *Acta Apostolicae Sedis (AAS),* 22 (1930), 563.

6. *AAS,* 43 (1951), 838–39.

7. *AAS,* 43 (1951), 857.

8. *AAS,* 50 (1958), 735–36.

9. *AAS,* 46 (1954), 589.

10. Walter Abbott, S.J., ed., *The Documents of Vatican II* (New York: America Press, 1966), p. 294.

11. For example, Paul Ramsey, *War and the Christian Conscience,* pp. 34–59.

12. Cf. Peter Harris, *et al., On Human Life* (London: Billing & Sons, 1968), p. 129. This book gives both the Latin text and an English translation.

13. *Ethical and Religious Directives for Catholic Health Facilities* (Washington: United States Catholic Conference, 1971), p. 4.

14. Earlier the distinction had been challenged by authors such as Joseph Fletcher, *Morals and Medicine* (Boston: Beacon Press, 1954), and Glanville Williams, *The Sanctity of Life and the Criminal Law* (New York: Alfred A. Knopf, 1951).

15. P. Knauer, S.J., "The Hermeneutic Function of the Principle of Double Effect," *Natural Law Forum,* 12 (1967), 132-62. This is a revised version of his earlier article in *Nouvelle revue théologique,* "La détermination du bien et du mal moral par le principe du double effet," 87 (1965), 356-76.

16. Charles Curran, *A New Look at Christian Morality* (Notre Dame: Fides, 1970), pp. 237ff.

17. Knauer, *loc. cit.,* p. 141.

18. P. Knauer, S.J., "Überlegungen zur moral-theologischen Prinzipienlehre der Enzyklika 'Humanae vitae'," *Theologie und Philosophie,* 45 (1970), 73.

19. Knauer, "The Hermeneutic Function of the Principle of Double Effect," 161.

20. G. Kelly, S.J., *Medico-Moral Problems,* p. 4.

21. Grisez, *loc. cit.,* p. 331.

22. *Ibid.*

23. Cf. *ibid.,* and Noonan's footnote question to Knauer in "The Hermeneutic Function of the Principle of the Double Effect," 162.

24. William Van der Marck, *Toward a Christian Ethic: A Renewal of Moral Theology* (Westminster: Newman Press, 1967).

25. *Ibid.*, p. 61.

26. *Ibid.*, p. 54.

27. *Ibid.*, p. 56. The sweeping character of Van der Marck's statement must be denied. Otherwise traditional theology would have proscribed all taking of another's property, all falsehood, all killing, etc. Obviously it did not.

28. *Ibid.*, p. 59.

29. *Ibid.*, p. 58.

30. This is a point of view expressed recently by Nicholas Crotty, C.P., in "Conscience and Conflict," *Theological Studies,* 32 (1971), 208-232. Cf. my critique in "Notes on Moral Theology," *Theological Studies,* 33 (1972), 68-119, 79-86.

31. Van der Marck, *loc. cit.*, p. 61.

32. *Ibid.*

33. Cornelius Van der Poel, "The Principle of Double Effect," in *Absolutes in Moral Theology,* ed. by Charles Curran (Washington: Corpus Books, 1968), pp. 186-210.

34. *Ibid.*, p. 193.

35. *Ibid.*, p. 194. Cf. also Joseph Fuchs, "The Absoluteness of Moral Terms," *Gregorianum,* 52 (1971), 415-458.

36. Where Van der Poel says "totality," Van der Marck speaks of "immediate implications" and Grisez (cf. below) of "indivisible aspects."

37. Van der Poel, *loc. cit.*, p. 201. Cf. also Fuchs above.

38. *Ibid.*, p. 209.

39. *Ibid.*, p. 198.

40. *Ibid.*, p. 198.

41. *Ibid.*, p. 207.

42. *Ibid.*, p. 210.

43. *Ibid.*, p. 201.

44. Philippa Foot, "The Problem of Abortion and the Doctrine of the Double Effect," in *Moral Problems*, ed. by James Rachels (New York: Harper and Row, 1971), pp. 29-41. The essay appeared originally in *Oxford Review*, 5 (1967), 5-15.

45. Germain Grisez, *Abortion: the Myths, the Realities and the Arguments*, pp. 307-346.

46. *Ibid.*, p. 314.

47. *Ibid.*, p. 315.

48. *Ibid.*, p. 333.

49. *Ibid.*, p. 340.

50. *Ibid.*, p. 329.

51. Stanley Hauerwas, "Abortion and Normative Ethics" *Cross Currents* (Fall, 1971), 399-414, at 414. This is a very thoughtful critique of the work of Daniel Callahan and G. Grisez on abortion.

52. Grisez, *loc. cit.*, p. 340.

53. This does not imply that direct and indirect are indistinguishable realities and morally irrelevant. It merely means, as I shall argue later, that both forms of intention are subject to a teleological judgment.

54. Hauerwas, *loc. cit.*, 413.

55. Bruno Schüller, S.J., "Direkte Tötung–indirekte Tötung," *Theologie und Philosophie*, 47 (1972), 341–357.

56. Cf. Richard A. McCormick, S.J. "Notes on Moral Theology," *Theological Studies*, 33 (1972), 71.

57. I say "partially" because even a disvalue which has no necessary causal relation to the good can be, perversely indeed, desired.

58. *Summa Theologiae*, II–II, q. 64, a. 7.

59. M. Zalba, S.J., *Theologiae Moralis Summa*, II (Madrid: La Editorial Catolica, 1953), 272.

60. *Ibid.*, 278.

61. Cf. Ambrogio Valsecchi, *Controversy* (Washington: Corpus Books, 1968), pp. 26–36. Valsecchi presents a thorough bibliography in this "test case" and digests the relevant articles fairly.

62. Edwin Healy, S.J., *Medical Ethics* (Chicago: Loyola University Press, 1956), p. 179.

63. Donald Evans, "Paul Ramsey on Exceptionless Moral Rules," *The American Journal of Jurisprudence*, 16 (1971), 184–214, at 209.

64. Joseph L. Allen, "The Relation of Strategy and Morality," *Ethics*, 72 (1963), 167–178, at 173.

65. *Ibid.*, 171–72.

66. Charles E. Curran, *A New Look at Christian Morality*, p. 239.

67. This monograph was composed at and supported by the Kennedy Center for Bioethics, Georgetown University, Washington, D.C.

The Pere Marquette Theology Lectures

1969: "The Authority for Authority,"
by Quentin Quesnell
Professor of Theology at
Marquette University

1970: "Mystery and Truth,"
by John Macquarrie
Professor of Theology at
Union Theological Seminary, New York

1971: "Doctrinal Pluralism,"
by Bernard Lonergan, S.J.
Professor of Theology at
Regis College, Ontario

1972: "Infallibility,"
by George A. Lindbeck
Professor of Theology at
Yale University

1973: "Ambiguity in Moral Choice,"
by Richard A. McCormick, S.J.
Professor of Moral Theology at
Bellarmine School of Theology

1974: "Church Membership as a Catholic
and Ecumenical Problem,"
by Avery Dulles, S.J.
Professor of Theology at
Woodstock College

1975: "The Contributions of Theology to
Medical Ethics,"
by James Gustafson
University Professor of Theological Ethics at
University of Chicago

1976: "Religious Values in an Age of Violence,"
by Rabbi Marc Tanenbaum
Director of National Interreligious Affairs
American Jewish Committee, New York City

1977: "Truth Beyond Relativism: Karl Mannheim's
Sociology of Knowledge,"
by Gregory Baum
Professor of Theology and Religious Studies at
St. Michael's College

Copies of this lecture and the others in the series are obtainable from:

Marquette University Press
Marquette University
Milwaukee, Wisconsin 53233
USA